# HALLELUJAH TIME

# Hallelujah Time

### VIRGINIA KONCHAN

THE POETRY IMPRINT AT VÉHICULE PRESS

Published with the generous assistance of the Canada Council for the
Arts and the Canada Book Fund of the Department of
Canadian Heritage.

SIGNAL EDITIONS EDITOR: CARMINE STARNINO

Cover design by David Drummond
Set in Minion and Filosofia by Simon Garamond
Printed by Marquis Book Printing Inc.

Dépôt légal, Library and Archives Canada and the
Bibliothèque national du Québec, third trimester 2021.


LIBRARY AND ARCHIVES CANADA CATALOGUING IN PUBLICATION

Title: Hallelujah time / Virginia Konchan.
Names: Konchan, Virginia, author.
Identifiers: Canadiana (print) 20210240075 | Canadiana (ebook)
20210240113 | ISBN 9781550655827
(softcover) | ISBN 9781550655902 (HTML)
Classification: LCC PS8621.O5825 H35 2021 | DDC C811/.6—dc23


Published by Véhicule Press, Montréal, Québec, Canada
www.vehiculepress.com

Distribution in Canada by LitDistCo
www.litdistco.ca


Printed in Canada on FSC certified paper.

.

# CONTENTS

– One –

Bel Canto 13
Joyride 14
A Star is Born 15
Schist 16
Desideratum 17
Apocrypha 18
Belle Époque 19
Hallelujah Time  20
Beautiful 21
Meridian 23
La Petite Mort 24
The Gilded Age 25
Psalm 26
Rhapsody 28

– Two –

In the Late Style of Eros 31
Fortuna Redux 33
Adult Entertainment 34
Memoriae Aeternae 35
Les Années de Guerre 37
Afterparty 39
Romanticism 40
No Exit 41

Lottery 42
Wheel of Fortune 43
L'Heure Exquise 44
Dead Metaphor 45
Information Age 46
Epithalamion 47

– Three –

Mata Hari 51
Zeitgeist 52
Eschatology 54
Coco Chanel at Prix de L'Arc de Triomphe 55
Stone Age 57
Golden Corral 58
American Pastoral 59
Fire Lyric 60
Air Lyric 61
Water Lyric 62
Earth Lyric 64
Night Shift 65
Les Fleurs du Mal 66
Pater Noster 67
Nocturne 68
Lullaby 70
Hard Night 72

– *Vox Populi* –

77
ACKNOWLEDGEMENTS 105
NOTES 107

One

## Bel Canto

Inside me is a black-eyed animal
struggling to get out, be free.
Inside me is a failed attempt
at explanation, a frozen pizza,
a botched murder, and a consumptive,
fallen woman heroine. It's not love
until someone is willing to die for you,
or quotes you out of context.
Agony: St. Joan or another
valorous witch going up in flames.
My transpersonal gender falls asleep
and has a dream it is invulnerable.
My metamorphic body falls asleep
and has a dream it is inevitable,
this slow slog toward slaughter
in the form of a ruminating cow.
Hand me my stilettos.
Hand me my Ativan,
my floor-length evening gown,
my fainting couch, my spouse.
Today is an envelope of money
I will no doubt squander.
Hand me my opera glasses.
I want to shatter a champagne flute
with my perfect contralto;
I want to discomfit,
then bring down, the house.

# Joyride

Go ahead, take it, the observable universe.
Take its buying, sighing, and dying rituals:
around here, we let the dead bury the dead.

That's the only way to get ahead, I'm informed:
buy into the urban myths of freedom and merit.
How lovely, how nice. My failed social utopia

for a song: your kingdom for my body's dark horse,
apocalypse awaited with bated breath but not believed.
I came into this world bringing only paper, rope, shadow.

I left riddled with compulsion, habituation, conditioning:
collateral damage of misfired bullets. Whose weaponry?
All questions tend toward rhetoric when one is salivating,

twitching: inundated by microsensations, electric shocks.
Poem as hormone. Poem as nostalgic aftertaste of affect.
Poem as necessity, vice. I will not speak if to speak

means repeating myself. Poem as traumatic wound
around which we circle, like repentant elephants.
What to enthrone as value: the human voice?

Poem as horror, libretto of organized crime.
The typewriter's carriage returns to the start:
all that drug money, gold glint on gangster dice.

# A Star is Born

Don't mess with a woman
from Texas. No, I'm not
from Texas, but I was raised
by wolves. In saying that, though,
am I appropriating the experience
of those literally raised by wolves,
as I was only using it as a metaphor
for neglect? Whatever. But really,
you're going to do this root canal
without Novocain? I confess:
I like witty people. I credit
them with having overcome
the shittiness of existence.
What is my greatest dream?
To become a jazz pianist,
and see money grow on trees.
It's the getting there that hurts.
It's the getting there that costs
a gazillion dollars, or its
equivalent in virgin tears.
When alone, we are all
Judy Garland, and that is
why I want to be alone.
There is no way to describe
the sublimity of music
entering a room suffering
under a gag rule for years.
If I can learn to do that,
my God, I will have won.

# Schist

I don't attract what I want, but rather what I am:
schist, a medium-grade metamorphic rock formed
from mudstone or shale, with flat, sheet-like grains
in a preferred orientation, often finely interleaved
with feldspar and quartz. Yes, I might produce
literature out of this conflict in my being, but
more likely is an ahistorical, silent trance.
I have lived long enough to see anecdotes
become statistics, like that line in the song
"A Little Fall of Rain" in *Les Misérables*,
when Éponine, bleeding to death from a
gunshot wound she took to save Marius,
says to him, in his arms: "Don't you fret,
Monsieur Marius, I don't feel any pain."
Just a dull clot on the stem of my brain,
symbolic of character types redeemed.
Who's to say: the general economy?
Swear on a holy book, curse me or turn:
I respect the rules of this establishment.
Ask any crystalline, tetrahedron form
how to value money, they'll answer—
far better to last, than to burn.

# Desideratum

Lies, like sugarplums,
dance through my head.
Like a heroine stabbed
to death in an opera,
my sciatica nerve
flares, then subsides,
before flaring up again.
Is a crime only a crime
if one is caught? Synesthesia
is for the charmed among us,
those capable of moving
between love and loathing,
or simply moving at all.
The last emoji on the list
of emojis is a country flag:
long may she wave, or reign.
I like it in my opium den.
It's quiet, warm, and dank;
I smoke until my poker face
falls flat on the parquet floor.
My human desire is simple:
to live on the perpetual cusp
of extremity, hour between
disbelief and ecstasy, having
been, and to be forevermore.

# Apocrypha

At best, life is hard. At worst, life is easy.
I only want to edit out the heartbreaking parts:
closeups of me on my knees, scouring for change.
Check out the pretty panties on that mannequin.
Check out the sound of ice cubes rattling
in my third whisky on rocks of the day.
Is that mirror reflecting me? The eighth
greatest mystery is when what is familiar
does not lead automatically to contempt.
Take marriage, for example.
Take the three- and seven-year itch.
I choose you, my escaped convict,
running ragged in the midst.
May someone prepare a hammock
for your body and drooping head.
I miss the church's indulgences,
the days of traditional blessings.
Pick up the goddamn phone.
The sun is an education, but
it will be hours until daylight.
May the road rise to meet you,
God-fearing, neutered by labor.
May you not die alone.

# Belle Époque

My life is a rerun commercial
of two men clinking beers.
I cross and recross
my legs, observe the
slow persistence of bugs
making their way across
walls, the Western plain.
Blush was created to simulate
sexual arousal, and mascara,
the doe-eyed gaze of youth.
I must be tripping. I am tripping,
on the red carpet between preface
and coda, anarchy of a bygone
era that may not have actually
happened. Why trust historians
when you have hyperarousal,
a leashed mutt, at your side?
I can't not give everything,
but then I run up against
the problem of time.
I only want that which
is forbidden; I hate
miserliness like I
hate toxic oil spills
in the Aegean Sea.
What rhymes with you
but the idea of ardor?
Winds of change, Ides
of March: deliver me.

# Hallelujah Time

It's hallelujah time, and I've come
to be healed from narcolepsy.
We wave palm fronds while waiting
to be claimed, like airport baggage
circling, indefinitely, a terminal.
It's hallelujah time! Our faces
are creased with worry and
our knapsacks carry weeks
of provisions, should the journey
prove arduous. Who is in charge?
The de facto pastor mops his
sweaty brow. He has grown old
on hallelujah time, is unsure
he belongs at the millennial prow.
Our pedigrees are irreproachable,
but that won't get us into heaven.
I can't stencil a blueprint of home.
It's like a pop vocalist's key change.
It's like being consumed by desire.
It's like dedicating yourself to a life
of works, to be saved by grace alone.

# Beautiful

Have a beautiful day! the barista says to me.
Isn't it beautiful out? comments a passer-by.
And so the day goes—and by day's end,
I have been told no fewer than 11 times
to enjoy all that is good and wonderful
left in our one ravaged planet, while
that same day, the Indochinese tiger
was declared to be extinct, 137 women
were killed globally in acts of femicide,
and flash floods took 150 lives in Iran.
Still, as my neighbor points out to me:
the dahlias are in bloom. Still, a local
rapist was convicted on all charges,
and a family member, hospitalized
for what they first thought was fatigue,
then encephalitis, and now lymphoma,
sat up in bed unaided for the first time
in weeks. You should've seen his smile:
it was as if it had dawned on him that
beyond what may or may not exist,
or only potentially exist, or exist but
unobservable to humans, is the mind—
its own place, complete with regiments
and cavalry. What if the day is beautiful
regardless of whether there is food to eat
or a kind face to greet you: regardless
of my appreciation or acknowledgement?
The day has no median, bell curve score:
no midnight pollster average to determine

whether it was in fact beautiful or horrible
based on the ratio of healthy babies born
versus those that died alone in the womb.
Have a beautiful day, says no one during
a rolling blackout. Have a beautiful day
said no one to the dung beetle, after
it was crushed underfoot by a man.
The plain evidence of daylight's dynasty
isn't enough to render this day beautiful:
like a lizard, I can sun on a rock anywhere.
Bring back virtue not born of religiosity.
Bring back buildings built hand by hand.
*This is my letter to the world that never*
*wrote to me*, wrote Emily Dickinson.
And yet, if she'd only waited until after
death to say that, she would have reveled
in letters, which is why death is so ironic:
only in dying does commodity value soar.
If the dead could be given language for
just an hour, maybe they too would say
*Have a beautiful day*, only they would mean it,
not as an empty expression, but a fervent prayer.
Thank you, cloud cover. You add up to nothing.
You have no shelf life, nor skin in the game.
When Narcissus died, Echo was disconsolate,
repeating what Narcissus himself said
before drowning in a reflective pool.
They were his words first, but she had
the last word: *Farewell, beloved in vain*.

# Meridian

I've been in this body so long.
My ace in the hole body, my one
bird in two hands body, my rut.
What does it mean to understand?
I count the syllables like coins. I don
my leisure suit and stroll the boardwalk.
O bituminous coal. O indiscriminate
largesse. My Ikea bookshelf body
is bookended by equine statuettes.
The mall is full of tall strangers
and I haven't seen a face
that loves me for days.
O moon, you are a hangnail.
O tree, your hair's a fright.
*Note bene*, this product has
been enlarged to show texture.
The cure's a subtle realignment
between one's inner monster
and the line of longitude that scores
the earth. I thought beauty would
save me. No, I really thought
beauty would save me.
I've been in this body so long;
I've forgotten how to flee.
Objects in the mirror may
be closer than they appear:
they too ache with cumulative
want, dead weight of destiny.

## La Petite Mort

You can get the popular vote, but what then?
It doesn't solve the problem of mold spores;
the unattended fair; the emptied pool; the din.
God, I miss you. I memorized what I thought
was your phone number: I've tattooed what
I thought was your face on my thigh. You are
an original, greater than the brands you wear.
You are the law's spirit; the lady of the lake;
the Latin word for horse, which is *amare*.
Love, love, love, that is the soul of genius,
cried Mozart. No, craftsmanship, said Brahms.
You savage me. You watch, bathetic, from
your high perch, stirring a vat of iced tea.
I can't see you, inciting schizoid paranoia.
I fall asleep in the orchestral pit. No, it wasn't
a grand mal seizure. It was the fine arts critic
in me, unable to take duende's absence anymore.

# The Gilded Age

The sky is all eyelid
and the moon is a whorl of cotton candy
with no one left to eat it but god.
When happiness comes back,
it comes back on stilts,
on acid, on bended knee.
Like a prodigal. Like a madrigal.
Like a boss man, gold chains glinting
in the harsh September sun.
Fate isn't just an ocean.
Some days aren't worth repeating.
I planted you in the fecund earth
then waited a season for you to bloom.
Slammed door. Hard bulb.
Vituperous species of regret.
You want for nothing: I want a window
beyond me, myself, and me.
Downriver is the past.
Downriver is the foghorn
that used to call the ship to port,
and which now announces
an empty womb, insolvency.

# Psalm

My first real job: barmaid.
I stood: I stared. I poured
cabernet: I dried expensive
wine glasses with a chamois cloth.

My first religious job: altar girl.
I held the Bible open for the priest,
and rang bells whenever he said
*This is the Word of the Lord.*

My path is set for self-employment:
after a lifetime in the armed forces,
I no longer want to serve the man.
Do I believe in corporeal punishment?

Hell yes. Spanking teaches us about
the utility of the scientific method:
diagnosis, prognosis, punishment, cure.
Another meat part on the assembly line!

But is it a boneless thigh or a wing?
In due time, I will have stated my case.
What are mirrors, cameras, even words—
the whole damn work of representation—

but the operatics of being, twice removed?
Language is other, and I'm without alibi:
museums kill god, but I will do no harm.
You're my imagination's sole figment,

curio cabinet of kitschy knick-knacks,
but just wait, I can turn this ship around.
Be thou my anchor, harbor, refuge, rock:
monetize me, on the way to higher ground.

# Rhapsody

I opened the window so I could hear people.
But all I heard was the wind rushing,
fine garment of nothingness, like tulle.
You sent me a handout listing various
cognitive distortions, which included
personalization and emotional reasoning,
and let me tell you, it was a scream.
I believe in the dream of human
perfectibility, however much
a vista, like mecca, out of reach.
In the meantime I have mastered
the art of appreciating objects
such as marble, which remain
cool even in sweltering heat,
even if objects are nothing more
than the decision of atoms
to remain bonded in the face
of travesty, poverty, and war.
In the meantime I have picked
up several musical instruments
then gently laid them down.
Can you imagine being lucky
enough to devote your life
to the high art of pâtisserie,
working tirelessly to form
stiff peaks of meringue?
There are omens to show you
you are dying. The world
is too much with us, first
as footnote, then as song.

Two

# In the Late Style of Eros

Loneliness is a female shark
who circles the tank repeatedly,

feigning interest in aesthetics,
before finally eating the male.

The pleasure's in not yielding
to prurience, or despair.

Why bother telling you
you look like a man I loved,

when in fact you are that man,
or at least were, in the

Pleistocene era of big hair?
Four score and ten minutes ago

I looked at your photograph,
so proud to call you my own,

as if you were my famous relative
when you're the stranger next door.

O, mealy-mouthed cliché.
O, catastrophe of cologne.

Welcome to our life
before it was lived,

dust bowl epic eliciting
no feeling but awe.

# Fortuna Redux

Eventually, an authentic feeling
passed between us: one of defeat.
I have a high tolerance for tedium:
those too serve who only stand and wait.
My fortune cookie: *soon, a guest will delight you.*
But guests are the most anticipated things on earth.
Generous, charitable reader, if we did not go about
interpreting chaos, what would become of us?
When I sleep, I sleep dreamless as a baby.
When I wake, I'm alone and afraid.
My opinions are public property.
Therefore, I will go without.
Our relationship is an orgasmic organism.
But when I hacked at it, there was no blood.
Being mesmerized is the last thing I recall:
the hypnotic sway of ancient money trees.
An accident is when something happens
that is not supposed to happen, and you
don't want it to but it happens anyway.
After you, I will embark upon a maiden voyage
and not return until my hair is long and white.
Like me, invasive species grow wild and free.
Unlike me, their passion is in ending:
the story, the composition, the light.

# Adult Entertainment

"I got you," the man in the porn
said to the woman in the porn.
Meaning, I won't let you fall.
Literality is a welcome relief:
acts of tenderness can occur
anywhere, even carnal scenes.
To be freed from the burden
of being oneself is a joy
rarer than orchids: a joy
only animals and thespians
know. Humanity is slated
for liquidation, which is better
than demolition, n'est pas?
"I got you," the man in the porn
said to the woman in the porn.
Meaning, you're not going anywhere,
anytime soon. In another context,
more idiomatic, *to get* implies
comprehension: a brief elision
between sacrosanct interiorities.
I hurl myself against the glass door
like a spurned employee, or lover.
It won't break. The world has me
in its grip, when all I ever wanted
was to be fucked, then left alone.

# Memoriae Aeternae

I love Jesus, I said, to explain.
I'll be your Jesus, he said.
Hit me, I said. He hit me.
Hit me harder, I said.

He hit me harder, dislocating my jaw:
I cried out in pain. He removed his hand
quickly, eyes twin wounds of concern.
It's ok, I said. I asked you to.

There once was a body, here,
and now there is no body.
What does that mean?
What does that mean, to you?

Sappho herself wrote of eros:
*it's as if the tongue is broken.*

We prowled each other
like cops and robbers
for weeks, static between us
rising from generated electricity.

So what if subjectivity is reducible
to performance, performance
to narrative, narrative to anecdote?

So what if I almost forgot
to call you my home?

The etymology of queen is prostitute.
The etymology of king is kin.

Muse, let me stay forever
in your arms: to the last
paradise, memory, let me in.

Lord of Lords, let me die,
and then, in dying, ascend.

# Les Années de Guerre

The past, yes, the past. Who was I then?
My inner voice is getting kinder,
but it's in enemy territory:
the dueling body and mind.

Life is poignant and cruel.
Why are you staring at me?

I'm not a clock, digital or analog:
I'm a marsupial born in water,
walked over by Jesus in Galilee.

But who's counting his awesome miracles?
I was happy peeling potatoes in the army:
happy with my ration of butter and bread.

*Dramatis personae*, all rise.
Court is now in session,
presided over by Your Honor
in deed and name.

Time is the essence of money,
which is why I fail at both:
depth over breadth is the gospel
I hiss, infelicitously, to the world.

The thought you have after the thought
you lose is the saddest thought ever,
and yet hope is the thing with feathers
that perches atop the combat vehicle.

Who reminds repetition of repetition?
What is the antidote to territorialism,
binding men to evil, like glue?

Me? I reject all domestic certainties.
I've never wanted to be anywhere
but here, at the apex of total war,
caught in the crosshairs with you.

# Afterparty

My body is the windmill you plow
through in a desultory game of
miniature putt-putt. Or do you
prefer the drive-in? If so,
it's the projector, hell-bent
on beaming crap movies
to the screen. Ungainly, this
trick pony the villagers deride.
My body is a giver. It hurts.
Bloodlet is obscene. My body
waits in lobbies, overhearing
nurses and administrative staff
speak of the deep existential
unfulfillment in their lives.
Song is gone, leaving just a lyre.
My body doesn't want anything,
save for Ovidian transformation.
It understands only one theory:
the thermal conduction of fire.

## Romanticism

The heart does its own
bidding, is more
than just a pump.
But it needs a storyline
beyond failure,
triple bypass,
attack. The bathers,
clad in sealskin caps,
dive into ice-cold water.
And thus the heart is
electrified, awoke.
Without a pacemaker, half
the world would be dead.
Art wields a scalpel;
science wields a knife.
I place a wreath of antlers
in your hair, declare
us forest and wife.

# No Exit

Past the memory: past the stain.
Past the rotunda which houses
the events of commencement,
marriage, licensure, and death.
Past the last installment, whether
of alimony, or a payment plan
for the latest must-have on TV.
Now that I have a Vitamix blender,
my stars are aligned. Now that
my husband has a rotating tie rack,
our unborn children can rest in peace.
Last night, I dreamed I snubbed
a famous writer, and when I woke,
I started to email her my apology,
before remembering the affront
was just a dream. Como te amo.
Je ne regrette rien, chérie.
Past the chocolate fountain,
past the lowest tax bracket,
past the sons of bitches who tell me
to relax, or behave. Past the ordered
rows of geraniums, into the door
marked *no exit*. When the waters
pool and recede, you are yourself
once more. Let us now sort out
the faithful from the deceived.

# Lottery

The bruise of this,
the wantonness of that,
the sharp waft
of garbage from
West 23rd street
and Fifth Avenue.
As usual, you search
for orientation.
As usual, I am
contemplating
the leitmotif
of our lives.
You call me
an old soul;
I calculate
the odds.
Pigeons do not
sun themselves.
Mere existence
is sufficient,
like light
divided
into wave
and particle,
or vision,
into cones
and rods.

# Wheel of Fortune

This world contains many worlds.
Why should the law of scarcity reign?
Money is symbolic value,
a broken palindrome.
I make it, I spend it,
and, like a dumb squirrel,
forget to bury it for winter.
Memory equals intelligence for many species.
Do you know where you hid that bone?
I'm not you and you're not me.
This is the origin of consciousness.
Am I a citizen-consumer or a child of God?
Can you give me a day without pain?
Yours, the face that tanked ships.
Yours, the viable pregnancy.
This post isn't performing well.
The manufacturing sector
has thought of almost everything
except the value of an hour.
Value me, but not before
a thorough appraisal.
Be the bodyguard who'd shield
my body with your body.
Carry me out of this club,
draped over your back
like a gunnysack,
and I will gamble away
my one life for you.

# L'Heure Exquise

I've hurt you: I've loved you.
I've vacuumed all the rooms.
I have no idea what became of us, yet
the possibilities for happiness are endless.
Once, when my lover betrayed me,
I greeted him at the door with a knife.
Now I am on my haunches, unvalued and unused.
Am I to be blamed for wanting absolution?
Am I to be blamed for keeping what I conjure
in a vial of formaldehyde beside my bed?
Admiring crowd, death is my downfall.
My students fail, repeatedly, to deploy
the correct conjunctive adverbs
in everyday speech. Consequently,
I fold my napkin into a perfect square.
Henceforth, the night ends so quickly,
bringing forth the vulgar day.
When images become inadequate,
I shall be content with silence.
When images become inadequate,
I separate the chaff from the wheat.
I feel I've learned so little, here.
The soul pressed flat is matter, unsexed.
The heart pressed flat is meat.

## Dead Metaphor

Fiction can sustain
the hypotactic,
composite phrase.
But I am a poem,
Lord, flyaway
cowlick on the
forehead of
preindustrial
man, singing
*Stille, mein wille!*
I rise, octopi ink
streaming from
once-webbed
hands, to write you
a letter thanking you
for capturing, flaying,
then releasing me,
fish gutted,
to the land.

# Information Age

What if we only get one life?
Who can speak to the
star-crossed lovers of
realization and latency?
Dear hydraulic pressure,
when I see a darting flash,
I assume it's a cloud or dog.
Life as ticker tape, fiefdom,
gaggle of mylar balloons.
Memory as stardust,
data breach, *cri de coeur*.
I am knee-deep in the
fallen empire of taste.
I sleep standing up
like a horse in a stall.
What is chronology
but a cog in a wheel?
What is immanence
but a long-standing feud
between entropic flesh and time?
The moving walkway is ending.
I lament until white-knuckled.
Your every word flung
from the incarnate earth
into the digital cloud,
as pearls are to swine.

# Epithalamion

Nothing sings so sweetly as silence.
My shadow lies atop your shadow,
eclipsing each letter I write.
After torture, moonlight.
After moonlight, grief.
There is no word for vanishing
in the language I painstakingly learn.
Samsara, satori, hyperreal simulacra:
I had a *raison d'être*, but gave it away.
For you, I sat under a yew tree's shade
for a thousand years and did not twitch:
I ate only lemons amid a welter of fruit.
Love and hate are ordinary amalgams:
the true mystery is bequeath and bereft.
To a happy phantom wed, until parted
upon death. Here is my living hand,
digits curled into a posthumous fist.
Enter the amphitheater with me:
to the usher, call me wife.
Hidden star, awaken me:
give me back my life.

Three

# Mata Hari

During the lobotomy, they severed connections
in my prefrontal cortex like a child rustling up
the last bite of ice-cream from a bowl.
All done. All gone. *All good.*

Firing squad, I am a free-floating agent
stripped from the putrescence of memory,
delivered into spellbinding feature films
without reason, adjectives, or nouns.

My heart's hot tears smart
and spatter on my shirt
like blood from a fattened lamb.
I laugh at my own histrionics.

Look who's laughing now.
O, lyric subjectivity.
O, exotic German spy.
Who knew you could quell a crowd?

My mind is an odorless vapor.
My body's fire-fangled feathers
wrangle five-star smiles.
I, Robot. I, Claudius. I bow.

# Zeitgeist

Death is an allergen, a foment,
a farce. Death is a handler
of turkeys and other animals
with grotesque physiognomy,
like baboons. Death hates it
when the mariachi band comes
to town—death is the wet fish
that stands on the sidelines,
arms crossed, while even
the village fool is dancing.
Vanilla custard. Hot dogs.
These are among death's
favorite foods, because
contrary to popular opinion,
death eats, though not much,
and not with any pleasure.
Death is not to be confused
with swooning or injury,
even though both brush
his sleeve. Can't you
just imagine it: death
sipping a daiquiri
underneath a beach
umbrella, scowl
affixed, while the rest
of the world frolics
and bathes? Death
is the patternless pattern,
the soundless howl,

the irritant that can't
be soothed or healed.
You live many times,
but you only die once.
This is death's glory,
the spirit of the age.

# Eschatology

Begin at the end,
forgettable trend
on a cybernetic plane.
Peel back the birch bark,
remove the plinth of elm.
Watch language blister
under the Pentecost's
glossolaliac flames.
Cure the cat, suffering
from distemper and fleas.
Horror, headwaiter,
is a matter of degree.
The incautious sunlight
burns out our names,
whittles us to a specter
of unsung, unknown.
We'll be remembered
by our good deeds
or lack thereof,
when reduced
to clearance items
in the eyes of the other:
piles, however fragrant,
of flesh and bone.

# Coco Chanel at Prix de l'Arc de Triomphe

All hail the end
of spectacle, pieces

of royaume scattered
on the sidewalk,

evolution of *la langue,*
after the fall of Paris,

from garbage
to decorative art.

I want to get to the end
of the story, the song.

I want a final death
in my bolero jacket,

poised in my front-row
loge seat, accepting

the violence of the
track: hooves pounding,

dust flying, emcee
roaring, life wound

of becoming-object
badly sutured by a quack

doctor on the plane to nowhere,
where I am instructed to enjoy,

beatifically, the end
of the sensible world.

# Stone Age

Awash in a pool of superlatives,
we forget the finer distinctions
between taxonomies. Look out
from whatever vantage point
your living conditions afford:
see the recording angels
huddled over lost causes,
lists of speeches and deeds.
At dawn, the hunt begins.
At dusk, we pet our pelts,
retire. Enough moralizing.
Enough faux-urgency.
Cadence, in Latin,
means *to fall.*
Stanza, in Italian,
means *room.*
The cycle is complete—
impeccable attendance
of the sun and the moon.

## Golden Corral

A new epoch of war
is upon us, once again.
We sit down and feast
on a trembling fount
of mashed potatoes,
sides cascading with gravy,
watermelon, rice pudding,
buttered noodles, corn.
It's buffet-style.
Bodies hum as they
deliver themselves
to the altar of repast.
These days, language
is a bare expedient,
a thing that hastens
the arrival of a thing.
We pay at the front.
Outside the franchise
is a wooden barrel
teeming with flowers.
The chrysanthemums
open their opera throats:
prima donnas waiting
for the rain to come
thundering, like the idea
of devolution, down.

# American Pastoral

Lo, how a rose e'er blooming
just beyond the camera lens,
a wildlife habitat protected
from Pinterest and Twitter.
If all life is suffering
according to Buddhists,
is death then sublime?
There, there, we'll wear
Noh masks and forego
eating, like supermodels.
Each morsel will become
an object of contemplation
rather than fuel for a body
already long past its prime.
I fell in love with my fifteen-
year-old self of late, but she
is also long dead, like Melville,
and all the Great White Men.
Let us now praise famous
hipsters, riding shotgun
in a Camaro with God.

# Fire Lyric

O smoldering tongue,
gallery docent of ash.
You are an outbreak,
asphyxiating the air.
Shall we gather
at the river to
escape you,
singing hymns
about your insatiable
heart? Barbiturate
to the vein, you
destroy what
is fragile in us,
our trophy case
of memorabilia.
How can I rest
when you quiver
in our midst,
by a glass bell
restrained?
All the guns fire
toward heaven.
Your purifying rage
cannot be consumed
nor contained.

# Air Lyric

Once I was a 4-H winner,
cosseted, groomed, plumed.
Now I am emptied of oxygen,
shattered like a birthing pelvis
on the factory's threshing floor.
I watch you watch tennis,
see the small neon ball
soaring when struck
by an agile queen.
Open your mouth,
let the vocable resound
in imitation of *Paris Spleen.*
Freedom's just another word
for something left to lose.
I'll become myself again,
consummate my love
not by taking flight,
but by staying among
you, like Jesus after
his ascension
could not do.

# Water Lyric

Lapidary blue, you
fall from great heights
to gently baptize
monk fruit strewn
on the forest floor.
Your ions tug
me through the
slough of midday;
your moisture keeps
my lipid barrier strong.
Aluminum, ammonia,
uranium and lead:
you are still pools
covered in scum
wherein lies the disease
of Lyme, and you are
hydroelectricity, tidal
turbines converting
currents across rocks
you eventually smooth.
After long centuries of
saturnine sleep, I enter
the canal, which leads
to the ocean. Beneath
it all, patient pulsing
of gondolier oars:

your hypnotic power
the silent worm curled
in a bottomless bottle
of el Jimador.

# Earth Lyric

Milkweed, thistle.
A plant that grows
only when shunned.
Would a feral animal
force another feral animal
on a gangplank, or to strip
its defenses for show, for fun?
Look around. There's so few rules
to hang gliding; it's all about the feel.
There is something droll about the
human endeavor, our destruction
of eight different habitats, then
backpedaling attempts to heal.
Flowers heavy with theology.
Erstwhile prophets of doom.
I know what my problem is:
global thinking, insufficient data.
Let's you and I be paramours.
Let's put a woman on the moon.

# Night Shift

Do you know Excel? We need a spreadsheet,
a game plan, a modus operandi that actually
fucking works, in the vast vomitorium
that is the failed dream of progress.
Greco-Roman culture, you gave birth
to Hellenism and coliseums, temples
in Doric, Ionic, and Corinthian styles,
but what has become of your virility?
I look to the constellations, stars like
punch holes in the sky. A little light
dribbles through. I couldn't catch it.
Hence, demotion. Hence, underemployment
and imposter syndrome in the land of vendettas.
I'm so sick of sycophants, of feigned elan. I am lost
in the underwood between sentence and sentience,
unafraid of gravity's swan song. Put away your
bully stick, already. I'm just going to sit here
stoically, until gripped by otherworldly feeling.
When it doesn't come, I'll turn on you like a
junkyard dog. Pity us our impotence, God.
Pity us, we have no one to whom to belong.

# Les Fleurs du Mal

There is a difference between charity and clarity.
There is a difference between mimesis and god.
Contingency, contingency: who can bear
the cruelty of winter, that consummate
*objet d'art*? I am still glued to myself.
Meditation hasn't worked, nor religion,
useless homilies resounding in the ear.
That machine won't do what I tell it to do.
That machine is working so hard.
In retrospect, it hurts plants to flower:
hurts them even worse to go to seed.
How long has your body been dead?
What was the name of the field?
I write your name in cursive:
I run my fingers through your snarled hair.
Incorporeal Lord, I promise to become fit
for human consumption. I promise
to give up this gigantic barge of sadness,
book of death I will never understand.
Beloved, I should have called you fire,
because you are not allowed and cannot last.
Seeing you, I want no other life,
but to die like that, in your hands.

## Pater Noster

Father, Prime Mover, God Almighty—
I have forgotten what to call you.
I have forgotten my pretense,
my sounding board, my ruin.
My friends, are they happy?
My enemies, are they fed?
O lilting, liturgical lament:
your skull will have its halo.
My finger will write your name
in an alms bowl of dirt and ash.
Today, I have done nothing
but historicize my feelings:
nothing but inoculate myself
from rabies and airborne ills.
What is not everywhere.
I am smitten with the sun.
Bad Shepherd, leading us astray:
the minute the doctor says cancer
I can think of nothing else.
Cure me of ancestral longing.
Cure me of the need for speed.
I shunt my body into your whereabouts,
Lord, pray for the end of virginity.
I have grown wholesome and wise
in the interstice between centuries,
yet my soul remains morose and blue.
I fasted, love, while others were feasting.
I stood forever holding my hand out to you.

# Nocturne

I don't know what's wrong with me:
*kicking the bucket* has always been
my favorite euphemism for death.
Death: privet, a shrub of the olive
family with tubular, white, heavily
scented flowers to which poisonous
round black berries are attached.
Death: a dumbwaiter carrying
dirty laundry or steaming platters,
plunging down to the *rez-de-chaussée*.
As if in solidarity. As if in recompense.
As if our shadow selves gave a hoot
who's to blame. Death: litigation.
Death: a riding crop, steadily beating
my draft horse heart. Death, I'm bored
already, pulsing thrum of the taboo
no longer an electrocuting shock.
Death isn't cute. Death isn't a beauty
pageant, walls decorated with signed
headshots of the previous years' most
celebrated dolls. It's a sewer, only
sound the swishing tails of rats.
It's a dishwasher on overdrive,
seeking to remove the most stubborn
grime to the satisfaction of the evening's
sponsors: insurance companies and banks.
I wasn't born a cynic, death. I wasn't born
to prostrate before a thesis that purports
to encapsulate my claim. I wasn't born

at all, in fact, until I died in your clutches:
applause roaring at all the wrong moments
as you rushed to deliver your acceptance
speech. And what are you accepting?
Charges of reckless assault and battery:
bringing me to the brink of nothingness,
then releasing me into plentitude again.

# Lullaby

Now I lay me down to sleep,
I pray the Lord my soul to keep.
If I should die before I wake,
pony up and paint a smile,
with ruby lipstick, on my face.
Oh wait, I'm not the phlebotomist.
I'm not the funeral director, the coroner,
or the mortician: I'm the siren song.
Yet, I want an open coffin:
I want to make eye contact with the dead,
even though I'm the one who is busy
ascending to my idea of heaven,
a racetrack with penitent men
running around instead of horses.
What do you mean, what do I mean?
Poultry was once a chicken:
beef was once a cow.
That isn't reductionist or essentialist:
it's murder. Thanks for shopping
at Walmart! Please keep the change!
I'm trying to harness the high and the low.
I'm trying not to oscillate between wars.
A technophobe on amphetamines,
I disavow this century, yet the future
won't have me, nor will the past.
Thus, I wear flame retardant clothes.
Thus, I am the progeny of therefore.
Three cheers for causal reality!

Like Frankenstein, I breathed life
into a monster. I invented a person
when there was no person, before.

# Hard Night

Then came, with time, a sort
of deadening. Then came
the birds that woke me,
*dishabille*, while I was dreaming
of satiety, gaiety, the blood
of my bootblack heart.

People are people, but the world
feels elegiac, somehow, now.
If I perish, I perish, said Esther;
and if I am bereaved of my
children, I am bereaved.
It's déjà vu all over again:

the undecideds cannot make
up their minds, and our nation
must come together to unite.
Part of the problem is lexicon:
the different ways we describe
or experience the mistral breeze.

A tautology is true by definition:
it has no possibility of being false.
We ask from God what we ask
of art: to be changed. We ask
to be more than frantic bleats
enduring a steady rhythm of whips.

What is there to say of earth?
It seeks redress, but silently.
Who can translate the forked tongue
of the plow, the lathe, the scythe?
I am not a manmade implement.
This, the autobiography of a life.

Vox Populi

A is for amoeba, autocorrect of asset price bubbles,
aristocracy and architecture: structuralist design, as
distinct from expressionist rage. Avidly aligning my
printer page, I asked Allah, Buddha, Christ: make me
more than a copyist of Archimedean proofs, my skin
the airbrushed accrual of unresisting serial commas,
accuracy of transmission as amanuensis my glorified
secretary goal. Honorary and dues-paying member
of the actor's guild, I avow history's rerun, virtual
production of talking heads in airless chambers of
so-called state, *enfant terrible* tyrants violating
antitrust statutes until forced to abdicate their
nepotistic crowns. A is for Apollo, god of sun,
leader of the muses, fraternal twin of Artemis:
goddess of the hunt, wild nature, and chastity.
A: ambulance sirens screaming in A Minor.
A: ant colonies, a brood of workers, drones,
and queens who live together, cooperate, and
treat one another non-aggressively. Efficiently
organized, they nest underground, under rocks,
in a single acorn, or in trees. Alpha and Omega:
the first and last letters of the Greek alphabet
used to designate God's comprehensiveness.
A: ambition, aviary, apiary, archer's aim.
A: mark of excellence. A is for aubade.

B is for blamelessness, Sherlock's whodunit
hook keeping beehived housewives propped
up on one elbow past midnight, while their
husbands, laid off from the manufacturing
plant, snore steadily on. B: boring holes
into drywall in a modular, prefab home.
B is for belief, belonging, beauty, bliss.
Barcelona, Beijing, Berlin, Belgrade.
B, blasphemy of nuclear arsenal threat:
the space race, proxy and culture wars.
As if a bomb could destroy humankind,
our belief in babies, biofuel, bric-à-brac,
and the helium balloon, now busted,
of belligerent financiers, cartoonish
voice-over whiting out, for decades,
the braying, bleating, bellicose world.

C is for churches, co-mingling, clandestine thieves.
C is for circulation of carbon dioxide, gossip, memes.
C is for cutthroat corporations assigned personhood,
criminally seeking tax shelters, bailouts, and banks
in Luxembourg and Andorra in which to deposit
extorted cash. C is for circumspect lawyers with
careful enunciation and smooth, cryptic smiles,
holding court before the prosecution, witnesses,
stenographer, and crowd, watching from an orbiting
aircraft or cruise missile submarine. C is for CNN,
Fox News: rigged conglomerates, sating curiosity
in 24-hour news cycles over sensationalist lies.
The Commonwealth's catabolic rate races to the
spine's root chakra: then, sphinxlike, expels toxic
contaminants in its ascension to the cerulean sky.

D is for dynasty, enlightened despots in Christian Dior
waving dampened kerchiefs from a balcony, Dionysian
ablutions performed by Alyosha Karamazov, sainthood
and its double, demonology, inscribed in Dostoevskian
tomes. Be drunk always, said Baudelaire, Rumi at the
wheel, all catafalque and remonstrance (*"Out beyond
ideas of wrongdoing and rightdoing there is a field.
I'll meet you there."*) D: dawning of diurnal rounds,
dastardly elements in the periodic table (dubnium),
published by Russian chemist Dmitri Mendeleev,
that are highly reactive and produced artificially.
D: the decision we make to deal with drudgery,
stalled engine of the duct tear, which, if active,
would water, with delphiniums, *mes devoirs*:
to etch the names, effaced, on the graves
of Lord Regents thrown from windows
during the defenestration of Prague.

E is for elliptical machines piled up in basements:
a lifetime spent running in place, not knowing
a war against one's body, once begun, is an
unwinnable war.  Step on, *homo economicus*:
the surface is black and slick, like eels, error,
and the screen of Grand Theft Auto, paused
at the elimination round. E: electromagnetic
induction, static crackle after a lifetime spent
chopping logs for the fire and heating up of
*eau-de-vie* for a weekly bath, on the stove.
Welcome to the 21st century, currency
uploaded to subterranean speculative
markets and clouds: filthy lucre
passed between bankers, easily.
E: elevation, enervation, ecstasy.
E is for Eurocentrism, endlessness.
E is for elephants' ritual mourning,
crying when losing a family member
to old age or poaching: e is the long
vowel in *to grieve*. E: where I bury
what I adore in an estuary, tidal mouth
of a large river, where stream meets sea.
E is for embouchure: lips pressed to my
instrument, whether of brass or wind,
to create a seemingly-effortless tune.
E is for elegy: formal madness
followed by elementary ruin.

F is for failure of fiduciary funds
drowned at sea, despite lifeboats
and lifeguards wearing flippers.
F is for fencing, fracking, and
the rhythm of riposte, for fanfare
checked by fossil fuel economies.
F is for flirting, fucking, *faiblesse*:
the fall of Enron financial execs,
sentenced to six months in prison
for fooling and thieving pensioners.
F: fake news, dealings off-the-book.
Fantasy, fairy tales, folklore, fiction:
from *fingere* (shape, devise, contrive).
Feign, function, sixth alphabetic letter
in FangSong, Felix, or Footlight fonts:
the frenzy of *fin-de-siècle* dénouement.
The temperature in Fahrenheit at which
water boils: 212 degrees. The fever in
a room when caught *in flagrante delicto*:
lovers who keep going and don't care.
The self-forgetting of enlightenment;
a flasher exposing his junk to others;
the flavor of a flank steak served rare.

G is for gaslighting, the spell under which
you convince me I'm crazy for liking to live,
term originating from a 1938 play titled same.
G is for garlic, *allium sativum*, flowering plant
praised for its curative, alimentary properties.
G: gyroscopes, gastronomy, bathtub gin.
Green is the color of the patina that grows
on the surface of copper, brass, and bronze.
Garth Brooks, golems, and gastric bypasses.
Glamor, grammar, goodness, gavels, ghouls.
Genesis' fifth day, when our Gnostic creator
invented creatures of the sea, sky, and land:
God's female, according to Ariana Grande.
The final words of an auctioneer after the
highest bid is offered: going, going, gone.
Pablo Picasso's anti-war painting *Guernica*.
It is more blessed to give than to receive.
Gal Gadot in the role of Wonder Woman,
who went back in time to save WWI:
shapeshifter of flight and invisibility.
G: glitter, glow, gleam. Intimations
of a realm beyond this, immortality.

H is for hermaphrodites, stress-induced
haste, and Helios, personification of the
sun riding through heaven on a horse-
drawn chariot. H is for harm and hire.
Heteronormativity wouldn't be so bad
if we could see the other person apart
from idealized projections in our heads,
dicey plots starring protagonist villains
such as Humbert Humbert, loins on fire.
Halcyon heydays in Holland's Hague;
hair on the arm standing up; marks on
the body (tattoo, insignia or stigmata)
bearing down. Hera, Goddess of Birth
and Marriage in the Olympic pantheon,
was known to be jealous and vengeful,
but wouldn't you, as consort of Zeus,
legendary for many erotic escapades?
Hell is happenstance, chaos, accident:
design principles gone haywire, awry.
The worst pain a man can suffer, said
Herodotus from Halicarnassus, Greece,
is to have insight, yet power over nothing.
H: honesty, hypocrites, the hydrogen age.
Haberdashery, the hotness factor, Hafez.
Art is a conversation between lovers,
he said. Light will someday split you
open, even if your life is now a cage.

I is for iodine, Crimean salt caves
from the Black Sea curing your
flagging will to live. I: the angel
above our bed, morning's aureole
inviolate despite a lifetime spent
in the kiln, clay body awaiting
inspiration:  from *inspirare*,
to breathe upon, blow into.
I: a linguistic placeholder
protecting the prototypical
me from view. I immunity,
I being-becoming, I *dasein*:
irascible inasmuch as I seem.
Without stricture, no texture:
without texture, no book or
spine, no leaves of grass to
dismiss that which insults
the soul, that ingenious
machine. Autopoesis:
self-creation, production,
the dynamics of autonomy
proper to living systems'
topological domains.
Stretch, twist, crumple,
and bend: I, a colossus,
maintain high fidelity.

J is for Jezebel, history's hallowed
whore pattering down the corridor
in jellyfish sandals, demanding
three square meals a day and
a living wage, to survive. J:
jugular, what you sever when
my tenderer parts are exposed,
like Jerusalem sage, jewelweed.
Cut the cord, unleash the crankshaft,
let jukebox speakers swell judiciously
on the day the ghostwriter gives up
underwriting in a scriptorium for free.
Jonquils, jodhpurs, jumping jacks for
calisthenics, nuts from the jojoba tree.
J: juridical. J: it's official, we're about
to jive to Hound Dog, Swing the Mood,
Jailhouse Rock, Runaway Baby, please.
Hysterical realism and metamodernism,
satire, tragic comedy, encyclopedic novel
of *Infinite Jest* containing 388 endnotes,
some with footnotes:  authorial unease.
Make a joyful noise unto Jesus. In French,
if you're on your way, you say *J'arrive*.
J is for Lady Justice, blindfolded, with
only balancing scales and a sword.
Who could allegorize impartiality?
No one: the ultimate accord.

K is for Tennyson's Kraken:
cretin emerging, sans fins,
from a watery abyss. Klimt's
fame sealed with his 1908
painting *The Kiss*, housed
in the Österreichische Galerie
Belvedere, in Vienna. K: the
only letter to keep a straight
back while its two remaining
limbs kick and scream, a truce
between *hyla* (from the forest:
paper, fuel) and class struggle
of *Das Kapital*. Kangaroos,
kittens, esoteric Kabbalah:
Hebrew for reception
of foundational texts,
along four levels of
exegesis, the fourth
revealing its secret
inner meanings—
in a sphere without
secret, inner truths,
the infinite is lost.
Yet can be found,
made whole, in
the Japanese art
of kintsugi: repairing
broken pottery with
veins of liquid gold.

L is for Loretta Lynn, red-haired crooner
singing Coal Miner's Daughter to listeners,
about growing up on a hill in Butcher Holler
with seven siblings and her beleaguered
mom and dad, labored into the ground.
L: longing for permanence, a shell,
exoskeleton, carapace, peltidium
to protect one from nightmares.
Like a slingshot forged in hell,
until the past, present, and future
become a game rather than a prison,
barbed wire a technical effect meant
by the studio producer to suggest the
difficulty of passage, the last aesthetic
sin that of showing seams, and in life,
of obstructing a shopworn body from
leaving the factory floor of the liminal
and breaking through the shadowlands
to emerge among the cedars of Lebanon:
the limbic system, becalmed, no longer
activating the response of fight or flight.
Levity, Leviticus: how lovely thy limbs,
draped across mine in the roseate light.

M is for Machiavelli, Marilyn Monroe,
the market price of meth, monolingual
monopolies, and mass media's celluloid
icons, epitomized by Warhol's diptych:
silkscreen images of her mesmeric face.
M: morning glories, blooming from early
summer to the fall's first frost, in trumpet
shapes of pink, purple, white, magenta.
M is for the many manifold multiverses.
M is for milk teeth, moaning, militancy.
M is for the missing, lost, and fugitive,
mistakes, mutiny, mumbled apologies,
murmuration of starlings at midnight,
and Milton's paradisiacal epic poems,
composed through dictation while he
was blind, ill, suffering from gout, and
grieving the loss of his wife and daughter.
Mercantile ships took you away from me:
the mercenary impulse is a *fait accompli*.
When I visited the Museum of Medieval
Torture, I stood before the mask of infamy,
thinking of Mozart's Lacrimosa: full of tears
will be that day. Magnanimous, munificent,
malevolent: spiritus mundi and domini.
M: Magnificat, let it be done unto me.

N is for narco cartels, nipples,
nymphs, narwhals: mid-sized
whales possessing a large tusk
from a protruding canine tooth.
N: a nail awaiting its hammer,
Neosporin on a pulled muscle,
a gift given whether a child is
naughty or nice. Neoliberalism,
neoconservatism, imperialism:
N is for trying to make it new,
and then failing, nefariously.
Nature, natural, naturalism.
Nursing Rosemary's Baby.
N is for negation, negativity,
but also nasturtiums, which
are bright orange and edible.
N: *nom de plume* of Niobe,
who grieved for her children
until turning into stone, the
Weeping Rock of antiquity.
Nox aeterna, eternal night.
Off to never never land, as
Metallica sang: a fictional
island in Peter Pan, and a
metaphor for childishness,
immorality, and escapism.
Nakedness reveals itself;
nudity is placed on display.
N is comfortably numb:
depth study in naiveté.

O is for Orpheus, apostrophe: turning away
from the audience in a play to invoke a third
party, such as an opposing litigant or beloved
who isn't there, doesn't exist, or, theatrically,
is just absent from the scene: muses, time,
God, fate, or any other inanimate entity.
O, phallic wand! O opus, canonicity!
O is for ozone, owing, and ownership:
balm, salve, ointment of opioid dreams.
O: obstetrics, osteopathy, ophthalmology.
O is for Odysseus, cunning king of Ithaca,
whose name means trouble in Greek. O:
telltale scar that betrayed the hero on his
ten-year journey through the Ionian Islands
and lairs of Circe and Cyclops, *home* a bitter
tang on an otherwise oracular tongue, craving
oysters, olives, odd ends from an open kitchen
whose chef prepares oxtail soup for the return
of the wayfaring husband to the once-ossified,
now unraveling, like a peeled onion, Penelope.

P is for Prometheus, Pimm's Cup cocktails
served with mint sprigs pimping the rim.
P is for the patch over, the pawnshop,
winding alleys leading to the dealer's
patio door, where he squats, grinning
and spitting snuff, knowing you've
returned for a pocket of oblivion.
P: the pastoral tradition, an idyll.
P: the pluck you need to forebear.
Picture your life without me, then
open your eyes, imagine me there.
Pies cooling on the windowsill,
Park Avenue sedans, patriarchy:
P has a way of getting it done,
despite partying on weekends.
P is for positivity, purpose,
particularity. Abbreviation
for pence or penny, now
discontinued. Per diem,
per capita, perhaps, per se.
P is for pretty, a precursor
to beautiful, like plurality.
P: pleroma, the totality
of divine emanations.
Palimpsest, penance,
piteousness, plagues.
Plath's petticoats.
The porous page.

Q is for quintessence, Quaaludes,
division of a census population
or discrete quanta into fifths
for ease of sampling. Quixotic,
Quentin Tarantino's camera
in a highly stylized Western,
glued to Django, a renegade.
Q: quadrille, danced by
four couples in a square
to queer opera melodies.
Q: querulous quicksand,
slow death of the status quo.
Q: quarantine, self-sufficient
O bisected by a blade. A quiver
of arrows belonging to Katniss
Everdeen, cinematic queen of
*The Hunger Games.* Questing,
quintuplets, quandary, quince:
deed of sale signed with a quill,
made from the flight feathers of
a goose, swan, eagle, owl, crow
or hawk and dipped in ink, tool
of choice for scribes who favor
unmatched quality control to
pen the Magna Carta or other
treaties of questionable peace.
Quitting is not an option.
Quiet, this is a library.
*Quoi de neuf,*
*quelle surprise.*

R is for rationed goods, railways, riptide
of the roaring twenties catching fire across
New York, Paris, Berlin, and London, in a
respite of economic prosperity before the
stock exchange crash of 1929, depressed
state apparatuses flatlining a burgeoning
America: Jazz Age's strutting trombones,
sultry scat, Art Deco, disco, foxtrot, well-lit
allure of rummy, romanticized speakeasies.
R: economic regulation by a centralized
government or the market's invisible fist,
rebel cries of fiat and bitcoin currencies.
The infinitive form of attention: to pay.
R is for Ayn Rand's *The Fountainhead*,
subprime mortgages and derivatives
trading causing 2008's record collapse.
The US holds over 8,000 metric tons
of solid gold, the majority of which
is stored below sea and street level
on Manhattan's bedrock in a vault.
R:  ram, the ruling animal of Aries,
revered in ancient Egypt in matters
of fertility and war. Its horns are
spiral weapons, used defensively.
R: retaliation, Renaissance, Rome.
Good riddance, boom bust cycles
of inflation and deflation, equity
and debt: R is for relative price,
real value of a house made of stone.

S is for somatic pain, shellac of armored bodies
drying on the battered *Santa María* before the
letters blur from soot and rain. All aboard the
Pequod, hero's journey reduced to satiric joust,
sodden mates of Ahab shuddering after battle
on the silo's threshing floor. S is for sawdust,
soybeans, and other monoculture, commodity
crops such as corn, wheat, and rice: 442 million
acres in the US, not to feed families but the huge
number of livestock being killed yearly for meat.
S: sea lions, saber-toothed tigers, seals, snakes,
skunks, sloths, and sheep. Spider monkeys and
sperm whales, whose hunting was a major 19th
century industry, to make lubricants, candles,
and light oil lamps, until saved by electricity.
Whales communicate through echolocation:
listening to the sound their calls make when
returned from objects near them, as do bats,
who rely on active sonar at high frequencies,
not sight, to gauge their path and determine
the size, density, and proximity of their prey.
S is for sickle cell anemia, sideral glances,
*solvitur ambulando* (solved by walking):
Saint Augustine's way. S is for salvation.
S: suture or stitch, to close shut injury.
Spit it out, just say it: I'm speechless,
beached on the shores of simultaneity.

T is for *Tristes Tropiques*, travelogue
of anthropologist Claude Lévi-Strauss
through Brazil, South America, NYC,
reflexively beginning: "I hate traveling
and explorers," and tourism industries.
T: Tahiti's technicolor sunsets towering
over the 118 islands of French Polynesia,
once a site of colonial carnage (over half
the population decimated by disease in
1767), where vacationers now go to chill.
T: tantalizing, typical, test, tease, touché.
T is for telling, the minor god of utterance:
terrorisms national, religious, ideological,
revolutionary, reactionary, and dissident.
T is for Tarantella, hooped skirts aflame,
termites, tornados and teamwork, because
alone life is impossible. Together, more so,
unless tethered to the astronomical clock
created by Norweigian Rasmus Sørnes:
abstraction's tipping point, the Trojan
Horse of the apocalypse racing against
the *durée,* now exploded, of temporality.

The magician's ruse is understood:
it is ujjayi pranayama, victorious
breath, unbroken cycle of inhale
and exhale like oceanic deities.
U is for the turnstile whereupon
you realize you've been traveling
with the wrong throng for years,
lost in the Upanishads, usury.
U: unusual, as declared by
doctors and antique dealers,
on its path toward singularity.
U is for umbrella, symbol
for the canopy of heaven:
umbrellas were used by
Hong Kong protestors
in 2014 to resist police
use of pepper spray to
disperse the crowd,
who demanded more
transparent elections.
Undulate, ukulele,
member of the lute
family with four
nylon strings.
U is for utopia:
wind rushing in a box
when freedom rings.

V: signal flare of *Vox populi*
on lips painted a voluptuous red,
wax figure's walkie talkie veering
out of range before returning to the
sealed kiss of a people's vernacular.
V formation: the symmetric shape
of flight for migratory birds and
military planes, to improve fuel
efficiency. All except the first
fly in the upward flow of air
from the wingtip vortices of
the bird ahead. V: vortex
surfing, otherwise known as
free lift from other planes.
V is for vespers, vigilance:
Virgil's vertiginous volta
guiding Dante through the
vernal equinox in spring.
V: Venn diagram, used
to teach probability, logic,
statistics, and linguistics.
Vitruvian Man, drawn by
Leonardo da Vinci in 1490,
inscribes human proportions
vehemently. V is for vandalism,
vampires, vagabonds, virulence.
In WWII, the Axis was outfought
on land, in air, and at sea, by benign,
more integrated societies. V is for
a vestige of hope: allied victory.

W is for Watergate, twisted arm
of investigative journalism finally
broke, wobbling voices of warring
politicians stuck on pitch of panic.
Clamor of complaint, meet euphony's
restraint, what appears beneath the
waitress garb: the body's webbing,
svelte ligaments of Weimar design.
Why is not a question we often ask,
whittling whalebone for the corset
of Wittgenstein's bride. Prequel
to Wall Street cons seen in 1988's
*A Fish Called Wanda*, heist comedy:
a tale of murder, lust, greed, revenge,
gangs, and seafood. W is for walrus,
a large, flippered marine mammal
characterized by prominent tusks:
they are tenacious, social animals,
killed for their blubber, ivory, meat.
Wishful thinking, wanting, weep.
Wherefore art thou, wunderkind?
Wave after wave of wonder, on the
head of a pin. Conjugating the whole,
as distinct from the parts: winning
isn't everything, unless you win.

X is for Xanax, xenogeny, and X-ray
photons shining excitable energy on
the pathologies of your lungs. X marks
the positus, topoi, key—hidden location
of the eyewitness to the century's most
moving testimony. X: fatal, declarative.
The hubris of Google Earth technology.
Let those for whom gender and speech
are performative acts sing of the headless,
stateless, and nameless, exiled in Xanadu.
X is for xerox copies of a ghostly trace.
X is for xenophobia, fear or hatred of
the other: the origin of all other ills.
Father Francis Xavier, patron saint
of foreign missions: in English,
ex means former lover, in Latin,
it means from. Ex gratia, animo,
novo, supra, libris, duris gloria.
X-factor: quanta of unknown,
concealed in herd mentality.
A parabola involves a point
and a line—the directrix—
a U-shaped mirror image.
An asymptote is a line
that a curve approaches,
heading toward infinity.

Y is for Yosemite, meaning "killer"
in Miwok: the name of a tribe that
was driven out and annihilated
by a California State Militia unit.
Yosemite contains five vegetation
zones, from chaparral to subalpine.
The forest is primarily coniferous:
the broadleaf trees mostly small
and unfit for lumber production,
with the exception of 550 giant
sequoias scattered throughout.
Several species, including the
grizzly bear, were extirpated
in the park: the mountain lion,
bobcat, wolverine, mink, beaver,
grey fox, long-tailed vole remain.
Y is for yesterday, yesteryear:
sex-determining chromosome.
In spring, neotropical flocks
of warblers, flycatchers, and
tanagers grace the landscape:
litmus of a region's diversity.
Y: yearning, forever young.
Y is for yoga: to join, unite.
Y is for you, the interlocutor:
receptive vessel, karmic seed
yoked to the matrix of night.

Z is for zygote, the event of fertilization.
Z: the invention of zero 5,000 years ago
by the Sumerians in Mesopotamia,
allowing for the development of
algebra, calculus, and computers.
Z: zilch, zip, zed, no, nill, nought.
An earth without form, and void.
White is the absence of all color;
black is the absorption of light.
Z: the signature mark of Zorro
who carved his initial onto his foes.
Zenith, fulcrum, epiphany, catharsis:
zigzag stich on the garment of time.
Z: rhizome, nomadic propagation,
intersex, interbeing, intermezzo.
Zut alors, she has emerged! cried
Lumiere, in *Beauty and the Beast*.
Fallen is Babylon, crooned Ziggy
Marley. Bios: lifespan. Zoe: life.
Zephyr: prevailing western wind.
Once you are awake, you shall be
awake eternally, wrote Nietzsche, in
*Thus Spoke Zarathustra*. What is great
in man is that he is a bridge, not an end.

## ACKNOWLEDGEMENTS

Grateful acknowledgement is made to the editors of the following publications, where these poems, or slightly altered versions of them, first appeared:

*Copper Nickel*: "Pater Noster"; *Yes, Poetry*: "Bel Canto"; *On the Sea-wall*: "Fortuna Redux"; *The Nervous Breakdown*: "L'Heure Exquise"; *LaHave Review*: "Lullaby"; *The Normal School*: "Epithalamion"; *Embodied: An Intersectional Feminist Comics Poetry Anthology* (A Wave Blue World Inc., 2021): "Les Années de Guerre"; *Radar Poetry*: "Hard Night"; *The Common*: "Beautiful"; *Massachusetts Review*: "Psalm"; *Alaska Quarterly Review*: "Les Fleurs du Mal"; *Love's Executive Order*: "Wheel of Fortune"; *Chaudiere Books blog*: "Schist."

### From *Any God Will Do* (2020)
*Horsethief*: "A Star Is Born"; *Diagram*: "Adult Entertainment"; *Free Verse*: "Apocrypha"; *Oversound*: "Belle Époque" and "Desideratum"; *Plume*: "In the Late Style of Eros"; *Dusie*: "Mata Hari"; *The Best American Poetry blog*: "Meridian"; *Tammy*: "Night Shift"; *Hobart*: "Rhapsody"; *32 Poems*: "The Gilded Age"; The Gilded Age" was reprinted in *Verse Daily.*

### From *That Tree is Mine* (2020)
*Jet Fuel Review*: "Stone Age"; *Queen Mob's Teahouse*: "Golden Corral"; *Clementine*: "Hallelujah Time"; *The Spectacle*: "Water Lyric" and "Earth Lyric."

### From *Empire of Dirt* (2019)
*Witness*: "Zeitgeist"; *Grimoire*: "Eschatology"; *Leveler*: "American Pastoral"; *Oversound*: "L'Heure Bleue."

**From *The End of Spectacle* (2018)**
*Columbia*: "Coco Chanel at Prix de l'Arc de Triomphe."

**From *Vox Populi* (2015)**
*Diode, iO, Laurel Review, La Fovea, Radar Poetry, Tupelo Quarterly, Wave Composition,* and *Verse* published excerpts ("A," "B," "D," "G," "L," O," "M," "N," "Q," "R," "S," "T," "U," "V," "W," "X," "Y," and "Z") from this chapbook.

## NOTES

The line "I came into this world bringing only paper, rope, shadow" in "Joyride" is borrowed from Bei Dao.

The line "At best, life is hard. At worst, life is easy," in "Apocrypha" is borrowed from Eileen G'Sell.

The German excerpt in "Dead Metaphor" is from the poem "Stille, mein wille!" (Be still, my soul!) by Katharina von Schlegel, 1752.

The line "All the guns fire toward heaven" from "Fire Lyric" is borrowed from Danez Smith.

The lines "We ask from God what we ask / of art: to be changed" in "Hard Night" are adapted from an interview with Jericho Brown.

Profound gratitude to Carmine Starnino, Simon Dardick, and David Drummond at Véhicule Press and Signal Editions for taking on this book and for the amazing work they do.

Heartfelt thanks to Heather Treseler, Sarah Giragosian, Alyse Knorr, John Emil Vincent, Kathleen Rooney, Eileen G'Sell, Jennifer Moore, Caitlyn Doyle, Sandra Huber, Nathan McClain, and Andrew Zawacki for their reading, friendship, and gifts of inspiration.

Thank you to my family: James, Theresa, Mark, Carol, Anne, Bijan, Camille, and Cyrus, for unending support and unconditional love.

Kourosh, my beloved partner and lucky star: you make me whole. This book is for you.

Stephen Scobie • Peter Dale Scott • Deena Kara Shaffer
Carmine Starnino • Andrew Steinmetz • David Solway
Ricardo Sternberg • Shannon Stewart
Philip Stratford, trans. • Matthew Sweeney
Harry Thurston • Rhea Tregebov • Peter Van Toorn
Patrick Warner • Derek Webster • Anne Wilkinson
Donald Winkler, trans. • Shoshanna Wingate
Christopher Wiseman • Catriona Wright
Terence Young